The
Homeward Journey
PATIENCE STRONG

The Forward Road

Looking forward stretches the mind – till it reaches out to find – a star to follow, a path to tread – towards a light glowing far ahead.

Look straight forward, never back. Then you'll never lose the track – marking the way of destiny – leading to where your heart would be.

Moving forward alive, alert – nothing will tempt you to divert from doing what you were meant to do. The forward road is the road for you.

Look at your Hand

Look at your hand. It is unique. Around the whole world you could seek – and never find a duplicate. Your life, your future and your fate – are yours alone, and only you – can do what you were sent to do – because there's no-one else on earth – has what was given you at birth. God's mark upon your hand you bear – No other soul this mark can share – or be what you were meant to be. It's your responsibility.

The Road that's Right for You

Be assured that you are on the road that's
right for you – if the gate you have
unlatched swings wide to let you through
– but when you find a gate is barred where
thorns and nettles twine – turn you back
along the track and seek another sign.

Seldom do things finish as imagined at the
start – but there's a compass in the mind
that leads the faithful heart – through the
gates that open on the work that you must
do. Trust and you'll be guided on the road
that's right for you.

Not Beaten Yet

Keep going. Keep showing you're not
beaten yet. Keep moving. Keep proving –
though things are upset – they're all
coming right, as in time you will see. It's all
for the best and the best is to be.

Keep praying. Keep saying the dream's
coming true. A wonderful future is
waiting for you. Keep working – not
shirking or running away. Don't drop that
burden – it's yours for today – so bear it –
whatever the weight of the load – it won't
break your back if you're on the right road.

Face It

Try to make a bad day brighter though the outlook's grey and drear – and a good day even better; keep the blue skies blue and clear – Make you weather. Bring the sun out. Make the effort and you'll find – You can change your circumstances if you change them in your mind.

Face the thing that now confronts you, not in a defeatist mood – but with thoughts that give you courage, faith and hope and fortitude . . . Though your fear may hover round. Outstare its grim and grisly face – Deny it. It will disappear and you'll see angels in its place – bringing good things unto you – and bits of heaven breaking through.

There is Something More

There is something more to life than seeking happiness. Seek its inner meaning and a treasure you'll possess – beyond material measurement, for you will have within – the light of understanding – so this moment, now begin . . . Search down every avenue of thought until you find – the light that lights up every hidden corner of your mind – with a radiance that outshines the sun at noon's high hour – and in its glory you will see the everlasting power – of a loving Providence – at work behind mundane events.

Laugh at Yourself

Laugh at yourself when you're breaking
your heart over something quite small.
Laugh at yourself when you're making a
fuss over nothing at all — failing to see what
is funny — and taking the pessimist's view —
laugh at yourself in the mirror and see
what a smile does for you. Laugh at
yourself when you're trying to reach for
the moon in the sky — and laugh when you
find yourself sighing for something too
big and too high . . . Laugh at yourself for
assuming that life would go always your
way. You never can tell — but all will be
well if you laugh at yourself every day.

Things that You Can't Understand

The longer you've waited the sweeter it
seems when summer's full tide flows at last
– the longer you've sat at a window and
watched the clouds and the rain driving
past – the greater the joy when the sun
floods the garden with waves of
shimmering light – the more you are
conscious of life and its mysteries,
morning and noonday and night. The
longer you've waited in shadow and
silence the sharper the pleasure it brings –
to watch how the blackbird alights on a
bough with a sweep of its fluttering wings
. . . The longer you live and the more you
discover the wonders of sky, sea and land –
the more you are baffled and silenced in
awe at the things that you can't
understand.

Nothing to Fear

What will you make of it? What shall you take to it? How will you live this new day that is here? Grey at the window-pane – morning breaks in again over a world that is ridden by fear.

Make a good day of it – so you can say of it – when the last rays of the sun disappear – You made the best of it. You made a jest of it. Armoured in faith there was nothing to fear.

On the Road

You can't expect to ride unhindered down
a busy street – obstacles and difficulties
you are bound to meet – accidents at
danger spots, obstructions and sharp bends
– juggernauts and long delays – diversions
and dead ends.

So it is in life – the road is rough, the traffic
dense. You come to grief if reckless or
intolerant and tense – but they who know
the way and keep the rules go with a smile
– helping fellow travellers, enjoying every
mile.

The Old Ways

A new road runs to the nearby town – all
traffic and deadly fumes – but the old road
runs where the birds still sing and the
tangled hedgerow blooms – with the wild
pink rose and the honeysuckle, overgrown
today. Soon I fear, they will spread and
cover the old well-trodden way.

Now tracks flash through the mind
creating a turmoil of troubled thought.
The aimless wanderer is lost, confused and
overwrought . . . Turn; rediscover the old
quiet ways, old but forever new – where
Nature waits to bestow her favours,
healing and blessing you.

The Good Investment

Time is Life, so spend it wisely; not on
trivialities – but on things that leave behind
a trail of lovely memories. Everything
depends on Time: work, travel, moon and
sun – tides and harvests. Time will not
delay for anyone . . . Time flows on from
day to day – but one day it must stop. You
cannot hoard it in a bank or buy it in a
shop.

Time is yours. Don't measure it but
treasure it like gold – and a rich
endowment will be yours when you are
old . . . Invest your time in friendships and
a blessing you will earn – Love pays
generous dividends and brings a good
return.

Thoughts and Words

Every thought you think and every word
you say – sets the trend of life lived out
from day to day . . . Everything that
comes, unhappiness or joy – affects you by
its power to strengthen or destroy.

Thoughts in time create their forms
externally – and build the dreams you
dream into reality . . . If this plain truth
were grasped and rightly understood – Life
would change, for thoughts and words
would tend towards the good – denying
evil's dominance – affirming Love's
omniscience.

Stand Back from Life

Accept the mysteries of life. Stop asking
how or why. Accept the inexplicable – the
soil, the sea, the sky – the stars that wheel
through space. Unsolved the riddles must
remain – because they lie outside the reach
of any human brain.

Accept the miracles of life: the structure of
a hand – an eye, a foot, a seagull's wing.
You'd never understand – so waste no time
in questioning, but in humility – observe
the good and beautiful . . . Take note and
thankful be – while you have the light to
see – before the shadows fall – Stand back
from life, reflecting on the wonder of it all.

Sunset

A day without a sunset making glory in the
west – is like a night without a prayer, a
bird without a nest . . . Sunset lifts its
golden lamp to light the dying day. Life
lacks lustre when in cloud the evening
fades away.

Where no sunset splendour flames night
seems to come unblessed. A sunset makes
the sign of peace about the world's unrest –
the gold and crimson seal of heaven
stamped upon the sky – breathes a
benediction as it bids the day goodbye.

The Homeward Journey

One road leads over the mountains through storm clouds wild and cold – another runs out to the sunset in a glory of crimson and gold . . . Some go by way of green pastures where the healing waters spring – refreshing the soul that has travelled deep valleys of suffering.

Good is the road that leads forward – to comfort, contentment and rest – and good is the road of adventure, pursuing an unending quest . . . But there is a point of convergence – where my road meets your road, my friend – for we're all on the same homeward journey, and all roads are one in the end.